SAINT ANTHONY
OF PADUA

CTS Children's Books

CONTENTS

Text by Silvia Vecchini
Illustrations by Antonio Vincenti
Translated by Simone Finaldi

Saint Anthony of Padua: Published 2009 by the Incorporated Catholic Truth Society, 40-46 Harleyford Road, London SE11 5AY. Tel: 020 7640 0042; Fax: 020 7640 0046; www.cts-online.org.uk. Copyright © 2009 The Incorporated Catholic Truth Society in this English-language edition.

ISBN: 978 1 86082 561 3   CTS Code CH 16

Translated from the original Italian Edition **Sant'Antonio da Padova** - ISBN 978-88-6124-019-3, published by Il Pozzo di Giacobbe, Corso Vittorio Emanuele 32/34, 91100 Trapani (TP), Italy © 2007 Crispino di Girolamo.

IN THE SHADOW OF THE CATHEDRAL

In the year 1195 in the city of Lisbon, in Portugal, a noble family had a child named Fernando, a boy who would become a great saint.

The house he grew up in was not far from the city's cathedral and his parents sent him to school there to be taught by the priests and brothers. Fernando loved school and made friends with other boys who were getting ready to be priests. He enjoyed learning new things but saw that the people around him were only interested in buying and selling. He was sure that the way many of the people in the town lived was not what he wanted for himself, and as he grew up he found that he loved the message of the Gospel and the priestly life more and more.

CHOOSING A MONASTERY

While he was still very young, Fernando decided to join the Augustinian monastery of São Vincente, just outside Lisbon's city walls. After two years there, he asked to go to the monastery of Coimbra where he could concentrate on studying. It was a long journey.

The monastery in Portugal's capital that welcomed him was a very important one, where Fernando found a large community of monks and wise teachers. Fernando was seventeen and was very interested in everything he was taught; he loved reading and learning about God and could always be found in the monastery's library getting to know the bible and the Fathers of the Church.

Fernando was a very humble young man; always concentrating on study and prayer, he did not cause trouble and never boasted about how much he knew.

In the monastery of Coimbra, around 1220, Fernando was ordained a priest.

A NEW NAME

Meanwhile from far away Italy, the message of St Francis of Assisi had reached Fernando's country and he was inspired by the example of some of St Francis' followers who had died for their faith. Fernando asked to join the new order formed a few years earlier by Francis.

Fernando, who wanted to take the Gospel to everyone and make it known "even to the ends of the earth", saw those who followed Francis as a shining example of how to live the Gospel with courage. So, leaving the Augustinian monastery, he chose to wear the Franciscan habit instead.

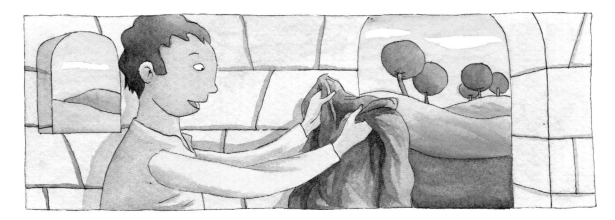

At this time Fernando took the name Anthony, like the great Egyptian hermit who lived in the desert. He studied the Rule written by Francis and left for Morocco to preach together with a companion.

Unfortunately, in that far away land, Anthony became ill and was forced to return to Portugal. During the sea journey, strong winds and storms pushed his ship on to the coast of Sicily.

Anthony was sad that he was not able to preach in Morocco, but in Sicily his strength and health returned, and God had already thought of another mission for him.

THE MEETING WITH FRANCIS

Some Franciscans in Sicily told Anthony that at St Mary of the Angels, near Assisi, a general chapter was about to take place. This was a meeting of all the Franciscan Friars in the world. The great assembly of friars became known as the "Chapter of the Mats". Because there were so many friars that they could only find straw mats to sleep on.

Anthony travelled to St Mary of the Angels with other friars. There he met Francis, took part in the chapter, listened, observed and thought about everything… all without wanting to be noticed.

The chapter lasted for the eight days after Pentecost; and when it finished, the friars left, each with one or more companions, and a new mission to carry out. Anthony was alone because no one knew him very well and they thought he was young and unprepared, nobody asked for his help.

In the end a brother heard that the young friar was a priest and so invited Anthony to follow him to Romagna. Anthony accepted and started on another journey.

Anthony arrived with his new companions in Montepaolo, a hermitage near Forlì where the friars lived together in simple huts. One of the friars, who had built a hut as a quiet lonely place, decided to give it to Anthony so that he could concentrate on prayer and meditation.

In Montepaolo they treated him with respect because he was a priest, but he did his share of the work to help the community, like sweeping the house or washing the plates. He spent the rest of the time praying or studying the bible.

A HIDDEN TREASURE

At the end of the summer there was an ordination of some Dominican and Franciscan friars in Forlì. The brothers of Montepaolo, together with Anthony, went to the city to take part.

Normally, some words of encouragement were spoken to those who were to become priests before they came into the cathedral and went in front of the bishop. This had to be done by someone who was known to be wise and understanding. That day, no-one prepared anything to say and in the end the superior of Montepaolo, knowing Anthony's skills, asked him to do it. Anthony was about to say no but all the friars begged him, so he began to speak. Everyone was amazed, because he spoke in perfect Latin, using examples from the Holy Scripture and the most beautiful and helpful expressions and sayings.

Deeply moved by what he said, everyone entered the cathedral for the ordinations. People were still thinking about the wonderful things the young unknown friar had said. He had shown his great wisdom for the first time, something he had guarded until then with humility like a little secret.

ANTHONY TEACHES AND PREACHES

Anthony returned to Montepaolo to say goodbye to his brothers and ask for their prayers, because now a new mission had been given to him. He had been called to announce the Gospel of Jesus to the people and villages of Romagna, which was a very divided and dangerous place. Anthony listened to the people and encouraged them and always tried to bring peace between them all.

Soon he was asked to teach theology in the city of Bologna. He was still young but his wisdom was such that he could interpret the Scriptures clearly and deeply. As a great teacher, he could speak to the lives of those who listened, whether they were priests or young students. Anthony became the first teacher of theology of the Franciscan order. Francis wanted his friars to remain in poverty and simplicity, staying in prayer near the poor and those in trouble; he was not so interested in them studying.

For Anthony however, Francis made an exception, and gave him permission to carry on teaching and learning. He knew that Anthony was humble and that his wisdom was a gift of God and could help many people.

Francis wrote him a short letter that told him to carry on, but not to forget prayer.

Anthony became famous for his knowledge of the bible and great preaching. Everyone went to listen to him and even Pope Gregory IX praised him, calling him the "Ark of the covenant" because he had inside him such a knowledge of the Scriptures.

iN FRANCE

Anthony was invited to France, in those days there were many problems there with people who believed wrong things about Jesus and the Church and led others astray as well. The Church tried to bring the people back to the faith but there had been many years of violence and war. Anthony instead, went with a few brothers hoping to bring reconciliation and a return to true faith through his life and teaching. He travelled through all of southern France, teaching, preaching, founding monasteries and bringing people back to Christ.

One story tells of something that happened in Toulouse. Anthony met a man who did not believe that Jesus is really present in the consecrated host, Anthony spoke with him but he wanted proof. He said, "I will keep my donkey shut in its stable for three days without feeding it.

When I let him out I will offer him food and you show him the consecrated host. Let's see if he recognises his creator without all the talking we have done. If he does, I will follow you and the Church." Anthony agreed and on Sunday after mass, he took a consecrated host to the stable. The hungry donkey was let out and everyone watched as he ignored the food and bent his legs and bowed his head towards the ground in front of Anthony and the host. Everyone was amazed and praised God and Anthony his faithful servant.

MESSENGER OF PEACE

In 1226 Anthony returned to Italy and was put in charge of all the friars in northern Italy. Anthony was loved and respected by his brothers and he was praised for bringing peace between the religious orders like the new Franciscans and the older Dominican and Augustinian ones. He also became known for helping divided and angry families to forgive each other.

Anthony went back to Assisi in 1230. The body of St Francis, who died in 1226, was moved to a basilica there built in his honour. Anthony was released from looking after all the friars in Italy, and was told that from now on his only job was to preach, so he could travel all over the country spreading the Gospel.

ANTHONY OF PADUA

Anthony spent time in Padua and passed the last months of his life there. In Padua he continued to preach and write books too.

In 1231 during lent, Anthony decided to preach to the people every day. He started in a small Church but soon had to find a larger place as more and more people came to listen to him every day. In the end he had to preach in the open outside the city. Often he preached in the fields, the people came and sat around him and stayed with him all day, even priests and the bishop arrived.

Padua gathered to listen, and Anthony's words caused fighting families to stop and thieves to give back what they had stolen, others promised to stop being violent and some sold all they had and gave the money to the poor.

ANTHONY AND THE CHILD JESUS

Tradition tells of many miracles that St Anthony performed, he thought of everyone's needs and wanted to bring them all the message of God and his love. Still now he assists those who are ill, he always helps families who are in trouble and does not forget those who ask him for help. One of the most beautiful stories about him is often told like this.

Anthony was in a town preaching and a man had given him a quiet room in his house where Anthony could pray. One day the man looked into Anthony's room and saw him praying, and then suddenly, in his arms there was a child. Anthony held the child with love and kissed him.

That child was Jesus, to whom Anthony had given his life, his preaching, his studying and his work among the people. Anthony will be remembered for his wisdom but his heart was always simple and pure like the heart of those "Little ones" that Jesus loved. Jesus was so happy with his faithful friend Anthony, that he put himself into Anthony's arms like a little baby.

IN THE FATHER'S HOUSE

After that great lent, Anthony, who was still young but had problems with his health, went into the forest at Camposampiero. He wanted to be alone; his brothers had noticed his tiredness and were worried. Anthony spent his last days alone with the Lord. In the spring of 1231, he became even more ill and his brothers arrived to take him back to Padua. Arriving at the convent at Arcella, Anthony died and went back to his Heavenly Father.

The fame of his wisdom and miracles was so great that Pope Gregory IX proclaimed him a saint only a year after his death. He quickly became known all over the world. In 1946 Pope Pius XII proclaimed him a Doctor of the Church. Wherever there are Catholics today people pray to him for help. He helped people who had lost their faith and now he still helps if you ask him to find something you have lost.

A PICTURE OF
ST ANTHONY OF PADUA

A PRAYER

O Lord,
Help us to be like St Anthony,
May we always search for peace
And live in truth and love
And bear witness
With courage to our faith.